D0297406

u enjoy thi

Harry Potter™

ALBUS DUMBLEDORE™

Cinematic Guide

SCHOLASTIC LTD.

www.harrypotter.com

Scholastic Children's Books
Euston House, 24 Eversholt Street,
London NW1 1DB, UK

A division of Scholastic Ltd
London ~ New York ~ Toronto ~ Sydney ~ Auckland
Mexico City ~ New Delhi ~ Hong Kong

First published in the US by Scholastic Inc, 2016
Published in the UK by Scholastic Ltd, 2016

By Felicity Baker
Art Direction: Rick DeMonico
Page Design: Theresa Venezia

ISBN 978 1407 17314 6

Printed and bound in Germany

2 4 6 8 10 9 7 5 3 1

Papers used by Scholastic Children's Books are made from
wood grown in sustainable forests.

www.scholastic.co.uk

Contents

Film Beginnings

Albus Dumbledore is one of the most powerful wizards in the world. He studied at Hogwarts School of Witchcraft and Wizardry and went on to become a professor and then Headmaster at Hogwarts.

Albus Percival Wulfric Brian Dumbledore was born in the late nineteenth century. His parents, Percival and Kendra Dumbledore, were both wizards. Albus had a younger brother, Aberforth, and sister, Ariana.

Albus Dumbledore many years before meeting Harry Potter.

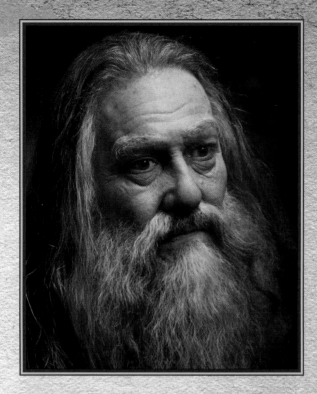

Aberforth
Dumbledore

Ariana
Dumbledore

When Albus was young his sister, Ariana, was hurt by some Muggle boys. To protect Ariana, the family moved to Godric's Hollow, a wizarding village.

Godric's Hollow later became home to Harry Potter and his parents, Lily and James.

When Albus was eleven, he went to study at Hogwarts School of Witchcraft and Wizardry.

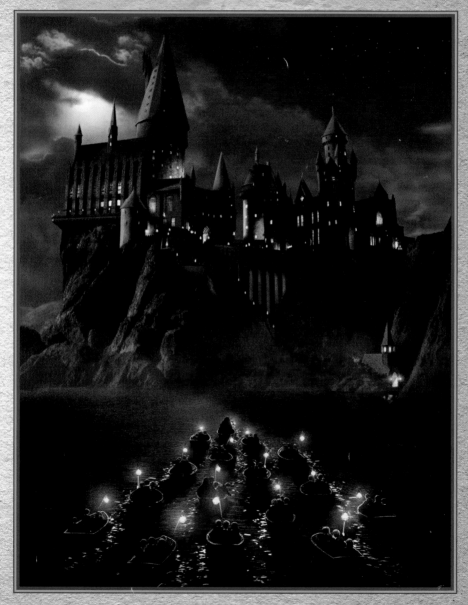

Like all his fellow students, Albus would call Hogwarts his home while he studied there.

After finishing school, Albus planned to travel the world. But his mother died, so he returned home to care for his brother and sister. There he met Gellert Grindelwald, another young wizard, and the two became fast friends.

Albus Dumbledore (left) with
Gellert Grindelwald (right).

The two young men were obsessed with the Deathly Hallows, three all-powerful magical objects said to make the owner master of Death.

The symbol of the Deathly Hallows.

One Deathly Hallow is the Invisibility Cloak.

Another of the three Deathly Hallows is the Resurrection Stone.

The third – and most powerful – Deathly Hallow is the Elder Wand.

Albus's brother, Aberforth, was suspicious of Gellert's greed for power. The three young wizards – Albus, Aberforth and Gellert – duelled, and Ariana was accidentally killed in the fight.

Gellert Grindelwald became one of the most powerful Dark wizards in the world.

After Ariana's death, Albus blamed himself for the tragedy. He mourned Ariana for years.

Albus returned to Hogwarts, where he became a professor.

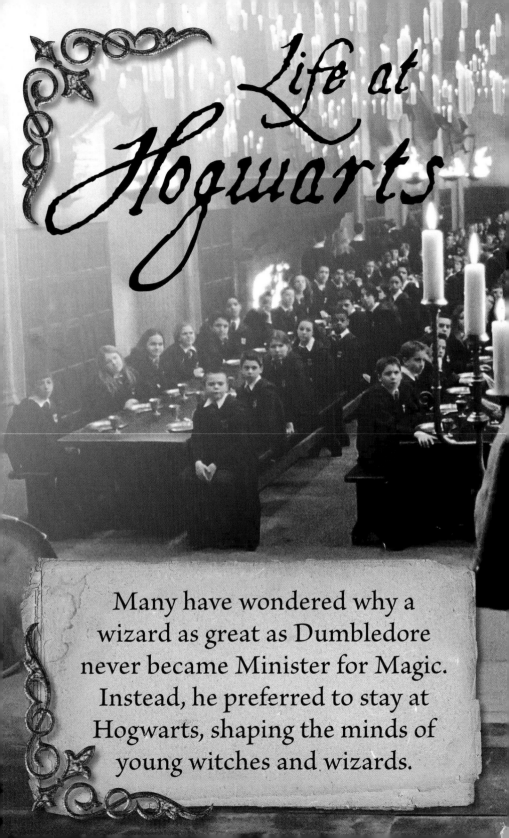

Life at Hogwarts

Many have wondered why a wizard as great as Dumbledore never became Minister for Magic. Instead, he preferred to stay at Hogwarts, shaping the minds of young witches and wizards.

The teachers and students at Hogwarts are devoted to Dumbledore. His closest colleagues at the school include Rubeus Hagrid, Professor McGonagall and Professor Snape.

Minerva McGonagall, Transfiguration professor and Head of Gryffindor house, with Severus Snape, Potions master and Head of Slytherin house.

Rubeus Hagrid, Keeper of the Keys and Grounds.

Dumbledore is so distinguished and well-regarded that young witches and wizards collect Chocolate Frog cards with his picture.

While a professor, Dumbledore brings a troubled young wizard named Tom Riddle to Hogwarts. When Tom gets older, he takes on a new name – Lord Voldemort – and becomes the most powerful Dark wizard the world has ever seen.

Dumbledore meets young Tom Riddle for the first time.

"Did I know that I had just met the most dangerous Dark wizard of all time? No."

— PROFESSOR DUMBLEDORE, *HARRY POTTER AND THE HALF-BLOOD PRINCE* FILM

Dumbledore becomes suspicious of Tom when a student is killed in the Chamber of Secrets. Tom blames Hagrid for the student's death, but Dumbledore is not fooled.

Gellert Grindelwald, the Dark wizard and former friend of Dumbledore, steals the Elder Wand – one of the Deathly Hallows. Dumbledore faces Grindelwald and defeats him, becoming master of the Elder Wand.

Grindelwald steals the Elder Wand from the
wandmaker Gregorovitch.

After his duel with Dumbledore, Grindelwald is sent to
Nurmengard, a prison in Europe.

The Order
of the Phoenix

There was peace in the wizarding world after Dumbledore defeated Grindelwald, but it did not last long. A new Dark wizard was gaining followers – and this evil lord would prove to be even more dangerous than Grindelwald.

When Lord Voldemort first rises to power,
Dumbledore assembles many witches and
wizards to fight him. They call themselves the
Order of the Phoenix.

A photograph of the original Order of the Phoenix.

"... the Order of the Phoenix. It's a secret society; Dumbledore founded it ..."

– HERMIONE GRANGER, *HARRY POTTER AND THE ORDER OF THE PHOENIX* FILM

The Order's headquarters is hidden at Grimmauld Place.

Dumbledore recruits many of his former students into the Order, including Harry Potter's parents, Lily and James, as well as Sirius Black, Remus Lupin, Alastor "Mad-Eye" Moody, Arthur and Molly Weasley and Minerva McGonagall.

Sirius Black was Lily and James Potter's best friend. The Order uses his childhood home on Grimmauld Place as their headquarters.

Order members Nymphadora Tonks, Molly Weasley, Arthur Weasley and Remus Lupin.

Alastor "Mad-Eye" Moody, Auror for the Ministry of Magic and member of the Order of the Phoenix.

Dumbledore learns of a prophecy about Lord Voldemort and a child who would have the power to defeat the Dark wizard. One of Dumbledore's former students, Severus Snape, overhears the prophecy.

Snape is a Death Eater, and he repeats what he hears of the prophecy to the Dark Lord.

Lord Voldemort is convinced that the prophecy refers to Harry, the child of Lily and James Potter. Harry survives Voldemort's attack, but Lily and James die trying to protect their son.

Lily and Snape became friends when they were children at Hogwarts. After Voldemort murders Lily, Snape is devastated. With Dumbledore's help, Snape dedicates his life to protecting Harry.

To avoid suspicion and keep Harry safe, Snape pretends to still be loyal to Voldemort.

Dumbledore and Harry Potter

After Harry's parents die, Dumbledore begins to look out for the boy. Dumbledore comes to care a great deal for Harry. He also knows he must prepare Harry for Voldemort's return.

Professor Dumbledore arranges for baby Harry to live with his relatives, the Dursleys. They are Muggles, the term used by the wizarding community to describe those without magical powers.

Dumbledore and Professor McGonagall bring baby Harry to the Dursleys' home at 4 Privet Drive.

"Good luck, Harry Potter."

– PROFESSOR DUMBLEDORE, *HARRY POTTER AND THE PHILOSOPHER'S STONE* FILM

The summer Harry turns eleven, he receives a letter from Professor McGonagall.

"Dear Mr Potter, we are pleased to inform you that you have been accepted at Hogwarts School of Witchcraft and Wizardry...."

– LETTER FROM PROFESSOR MCGONAGALL,
HARRY POTTER AND THE PHILOSOPHER'S STONE FILM

During Harry's years at Hogwarts, Dumbledore watches over and protects him.

Dumbledore gives Harry the Invisibility Cloak, one of the three Deathly Hallows. It had belonged to Harry's father, James.

Dumbledore and Snape protect Harry and other students when Hogwarts is threatened by an escapee from Azkaban, the wizard prison.

Harry and his closest friends, Ron Weasley and Hermione Granger, look up to Dumbledore.

When student Neville Longbottom stands up to Harry, Ron and Hermione, Dumbledore recognizes his bravery before the whole school.

"*It takes a great deal of bravery to stand up to your enemies, but a great deal more to stand up to your friends.*"

– PROFESSOR DUMBLEDORE, *HARRY POTTER AND THE PHILOSOPHER'S STONE* FILM

After Harry witnesses Voldemort's return, Dumbledore is one of the few to believe him. Many wizards, including the Minister for Magic, are too afraid to accept the truth: the Dark Lord is back.

"Dark and difficult times lie ahead. Soon we must all face the choice between what is right and what is easy."

– Professor Dumbledore, *Harry Potter and the Goblet of Fire* film

Harry and his friends form a student group dedicated to learning defensive spells to protect themselves from Dark magic. They name themselves Dumbledore's Army in honour of Professor Dumbledore.

Harry and fellow D.A. member Neville Longbottom practise in the Room of Requirement.

Fighting Dark Forces

Professor Dumbledore has
dedicated his life to protecting
witches, wizards and
Muggles from the power of
Dark magic.

As Voldemort grows stronger, he uses his connection with Harry to lure the boy to the Ministry of Magic. Dumbledore comes to Harry's rescue and duels the Dark Lord.

"It was foolish of you to come here tonight, Tom."

– PROFESSOR DUMBLEDORE, *HARRY POTTER AND THE ORDER OF THE PHOENIX* FILM

Dumbledore is determined to protect Harry from Voldemort.

Dumbledore and Harry discover the secret behind Voldemort's return – in order to become immortal, Voldemort has split his soul and concealed parts of it in objects called Horcruxes. Together, Dumbledore and Harry set out to find and destroy the Horcruxes.

Harry: *"If you could find them all . . . if you did destroy each Horcrux . . ."*

Dumbledore: *"One destroys Voldemort."*

– HARRY POTTER AND THE HALF-BLOOD PRINCE FILM

The first Horcrux Dumbledore discovers is a ring that holds a powerful curse.

The Horcrux gravely injures Dumbledore. Professor Snape confines the curse to Dumbledore's hand, but they both know that eventually the curse will spread.

Dumbledore brings Harry to find the next Horcrux, which Voldemort has hidden in a cave.

The Horcrux is protected by Dark magic. Dumbledore must drink
a poisonous potion to retrieve it.

The potion weakens Dumbledore, but he still finds the strength
to protect Harry from Inferi – corpses that have been reanimated
through Dark magic.

When Professor Dumbledore and Harry return to Hogwarts, they find out that Death Eaters have broken into the school. After years of being seemingly loyal to Dumbledore, Snape must now prove himself to be an ally to the Dark forces.

Bellatrix Lestrange leads the Death Eaters into Hogwarts.

"Severus . . . please . . ."

– PROFESSOR DUMBLEDORE, *HARRY POTTER AND THE HALF-BLOOD PRINCE* FILM

In order to fulfil a promise to Dumbledore, Professor Snape must cast the Killing Curse and end his old friend's life.

Dumbledore falls from the top of Hogwarts's Astronomy Tower.
His sacrifice sets a larger plan in motion.

Harry and his friends mourn the passing of their mentor
and friend.

Legacy

After Dumbledore's death, Harry remains determined to complete the task Dumbledore left for him: find and destroy the remaining Horcruxes so that Voldemort will become mortal once more.

Minister for Magic Rufus Scrimgeour reads
Dumbledore's last will and testament to Harry,
Ron and Hermione. Dumbledore leaves
each of the trio a gift that will serve to help in
the hunt for Horcruxes.

Dumbledore leaves Harry the Sword of Gryffindor.

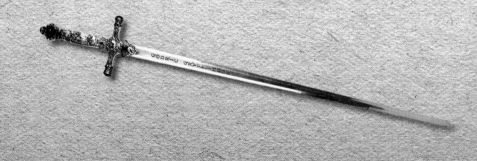

Dumbledore leaves Ron his Deluminator.

Dumbledore leaves Hermione a book that offers information for the quest to defeat the Dark Lord: *The Tales of Beedle the Bard.*

Voldemort becomes convinced he needs
a more powerful wand to defeat Harry.
He removes the legendary Elder Wand
from Dumbledore's tomb.

Voldemort uses the Elder Wand for the first time.

Because of his connection with Voldemort, Harry can sense that the Dark Lord now has the powerful Elder Wand.

Harry, Ron and Hermione discover there are more Horcruxes at Hogwarts.

Dumbledore's younger brother Aberforth and Neville help Harry, Ron and Hermione slip past Death Eaters and back into the castle to find the Horcrux.

There is a secret entrance to the school behind Aberforth's painting of Ariana.

Harry, Ron and Hermione destroy a Horcrux hidden in the Room of Requirement.

Ron and Hermione use a Basilisk fang to destroy another Horcrux in the Chamber of Secrets.

Determined to destroy Harry, Voldemort attacks Hogwarts. During the battle, Voldemort mortally wounds Snape. Just before Snape dies, he tells Harry to take one of his tears to Dumbledore's Pensieve.

When Harry sees Snape's memories, he finally discovers the truth about his connection with Voldemort. Harry himself is a Horcrux. To defeat the Dark Lord, Harry must allow Voldemort to kill him.

Dumbledore: "There's a reason Harry can speak with snakes. There's a reason he can look into Lord Voldemort's mind. A part of Voldemort lives inside him."

Snape: "So when the time comes, the boy must die?"

Dumbledore: "Yes. And Voldemort himself must do it."

– Harry Potter and the Deathly Hallows – Part 2 film

Harry surrenders himself to Voldemort in the Forbidden Forest. He allows Voldemort to kill him so the Horcrux inside him can be destroyed.

"Harry Potter. The Boy Who Lived. Come to die."

– VOLDEMORT, *HARRY POTTER AND THE DEATHLY HALLOWS – PART 2* FILM

Voldemort believes he has killed Harry, but he succeeds only in destroying the Horcrux. As Harry lies unconscious, he has a vision of Dumbledore.

Harry: "So, it's true, then, sir? A part of him lives within me, doesn't it?"

Dumbledore: "Did. It was just destroyed many moments ago by none other than Voldemort himself. . . . You were the Horcrux he never meant to make, Harry."

– HARRY POTTER AND THE DEATHLY HALLOWS – PART 2 FILM

Neville uses the Sword of Gryffindor to destroy the last Horcrux, Voldemort's snake, Nagini.

Thanks to Harry and his friends, Dumbledore's plan has been fulfilled: Voldemort is finally mortal once more. He and Harry can face each other on equal footing.

Harry and Voldemort's final duel at the Battle of Hogwarts.

"Do not pity the dead, Harry. Pity the living and above all, all those who live without love."

– Professor Dumbledore, *Harry Potter and the Deathly Hallows – Part 2* film